2 Barefoot Sandals   Seaside Coasters **4**

6 Lacy Cape   Rosy Head Wrap **9**

For perfect summer comfort and style, use cotton yarns or other soft fibers to knit any of these 10 easy designs.

12 Scoop Neck Top   Anchor Pillow **15**

18 Striped Tote   Long Vest **20**

23 Surfside Tunic   Fringed Hip Wrap **26**

LEISURE ARTS, INC. • Maumelle, Arkansas

Barefoot Sandals — EASY

Finished Size: One size fits most

SHOPPING LIST

Yarn (Medium Weight)
- ☐ 25 yards (23 meters)

Knitting Needles
Straight,
- ☐ Size 10½ (6.5 mm)
  or size needed for gauge

Additional Supplies
- ☐ Yarn needle

GAUGE INFORMATION

In Garter Stitch (knit every row),
8 sts and 8 rows = 2" (5 cm)

TECHNIQUES USED

- Adding new sts *(Figs. 3a & b, page 29)*
- YO at beginning of a row *(Fig. A)*

Fig. A

- YO twice *(Fig. B)*

Fig. B

BODY (Make 2)

Make a slip knot, leaving a 10" (25.5 cm) end to form toe loop.

Row 1: YO, K1: 2 sts.

Rows 2-6: YO, knit across: 7 sts.

Row 7: YO, K1, YO twice as you knit next 5 sts, K1: 13 sts.

To elongate stitches, knit only the first YO of each stitch, dropping the remaining YO from the left needle. Tug gently on the piece to even the elongated stitches.

Row 8: YO, K1, elongating each st knit across to last 2 sts, K2: 9 sts.

Rows 9-11: YO, knit across: 12 sts.

Row 12: YO, K1, YO twice as you knit next 10 sts, K1: 23 sts.

Row 13: YO, K1, elongating each st knit across to last 2 sts, K2: 14 sts.

Rows 14-16: YO, knit across: 17 sts.

Row 17 (Ties)**:** Add on 20 sts (**tie made**), bind off all sts, leave last loop on right needle, **turn**; add on 20 sts (**tie made**), bind off all sts.

Fringe: Cut two 8½" (21.5 cm) long strands of yarn. Thread yarn needle with one strand, insert needle through end of one Tie, remove needle. With ends matching, tie two overhand knots close to end of Tie. Repeat for remaining Tie.

Toe Loop: Thread yarn needle with beginning end, insert needle in first st, adjust loop to desired size; then secure end.

Seaside Coasters — EASY

Finished Size: 4" (10 cm) square

SHOPPING LIST

Yarn (Medium Weight)
- ☐ Red - 25 yards (23 meters)
- ☐ Navy - 25 yards (23 meters)
- ☐ White - 25 yards (23 meters)
- ☐ Yellow - 25 yards (23 meters)

Knitting Needles

Straight,
- ☐ Size 6 (4 mm)

  or size needed for gauge

Additional Supplies
- ☐ Yarn needle

GAUGE INFORMATION

In Stockinette Stitch

(knit one row, purl one row),

10 sts and 16 rows = 2" (5 cm)

COASTER

(Make one **each** with Red, Navy, White, **and** Yellow)

Cast on 21 sts.

Rows 1-4: K1, (P1, K1) across.

Row 5 (Right side)**:** K1, P1, knit across to last 2 sts, P1, K1.

Row 6: K1, P1, K1, purl across to last 3 sts, K1, P1, K1.

Rows 7-28: Repeat Rows 5 and 6, 11 times.

Rows 29-32: K1, (P1, K1) across.

Bind off all sts in pattern.

Using Duplicate Stitch *(Figs. 7a & b, page 30)*, follow charts on page 5 to add design in color indicated to Coaster.

SEAHORSE CHART

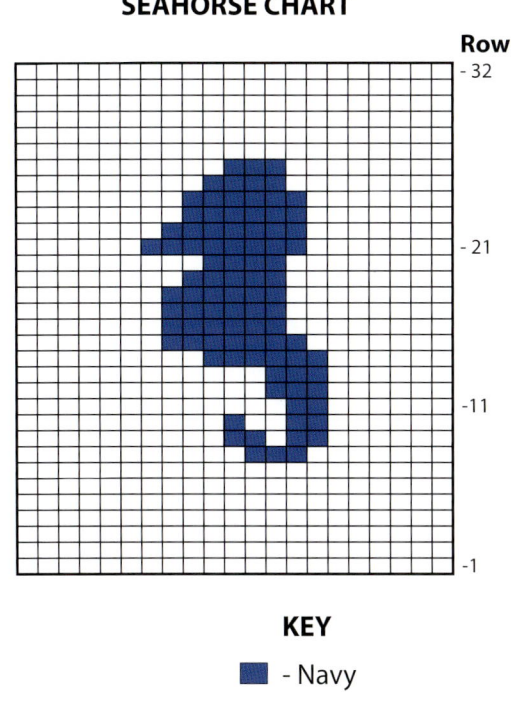

KEY

■ - Navy

LIGHTHOUSE CHART

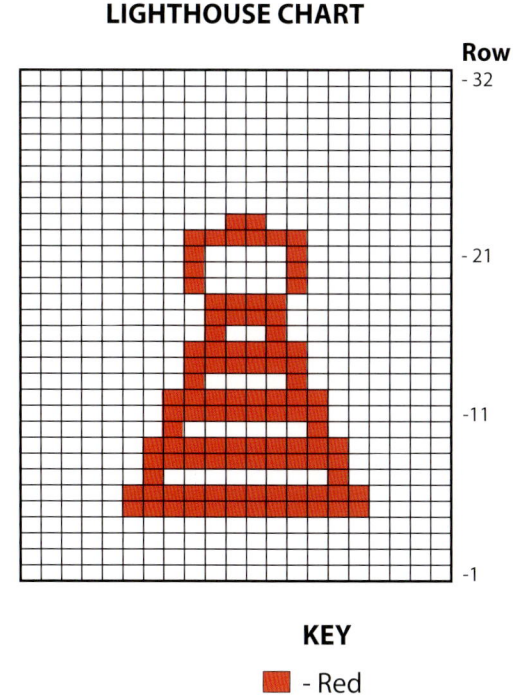

KEY

■ - Red

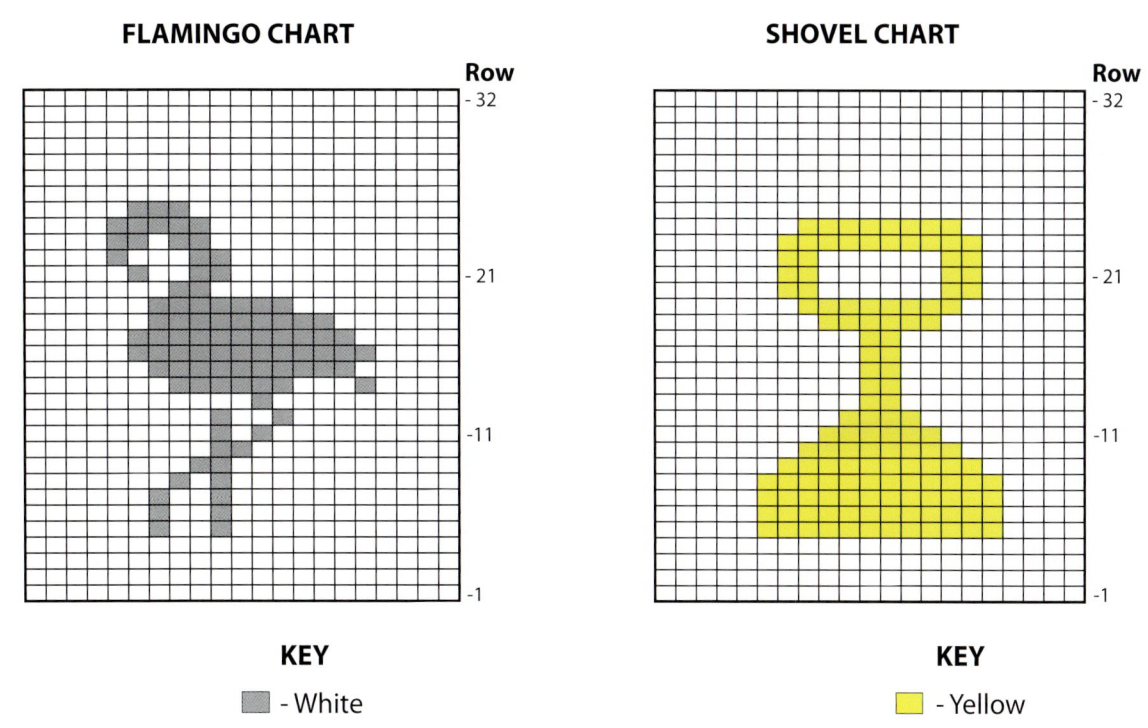

FLAMINGO CHART

KEY

■ - White

SHOVEL CHART

KEY

■ - Yellow

Lacy Cape — EASY

SHOPPING LIST

Yarn (Medium Weight) 〖4〗
[3.5 ounces, 186 yards
(100 grams, 170 meters) per skein]:
☐ 3 skeins

Knitting Needles
Straight,
☐ Size 10 (6 mm)
or size needed for gauge

Additional Supplies
☐ 1½" (38 mm) Button
☐ Sewing needle and thread

SIZE INFORMATION

Size: Small {Medium-Large}
Top Edge:
24½{25½-26½}"/62{65-67.5} cm
Bottom Edge:
45{48-51}"/114.5{122-129.5} cm
Length: 13" (33 cm)

Size Note: We have printed the instructions for the sizes in different colors to make it easier for you to find:

- Size Small in Blue
- Size Medium in Pink
- Size Large in Green

Instructions in Black apply to all sizes.

GAUGE INFORMATION

In Garter Stitch (knit every row),
   12 sts = 4½" (11.5 cm);
   11 rows = 2" (5 cm)
In pattern,
   9 rows = 2" (5 cm)

TECHNIQUES USED

- YO *(Fig. 2, page 29)*
- K2 tog *(Fig. 4, page 29)*

BODY

Cast on 120{128-136} sts.

Rows 1-3: Knit across.

Row 4 (Right side - Increase row)**:** K4, YO, (K1, YO) across to last 5 sts, K5: 232{248-264} sts.

Row 5 (Decrease row)**:** K5, drop YO off left needle, (K1, drop YO) across to last 4 sts, K4: 120{128-136} sts.

Row 6: K4, (YO, K2 tog) across to last 4 sts, K4.

Row 7: Knit across.

Rows 8-38: Repeat Rows 4-7, 7 times; then repeat Rows 4-6 once **more**.

Row 39: K5{4-3}, K2 tog, (K8, K2 tog) across to last 13{12-11} sts, K 13{12-11}: 109{116-123} sts.

Rows 40-42: Repeat Rows 4-6.

Row 43: K5{4-3}, K2 tog, (K7, K2 tog) across to last 12{11-10} sts, K 12{11-10}: 98{104-110} sts.

Rows 44-46: Repeat Rows 4-6.

Row 47: K5{4-3}, K2 tog, (K6, K2 tog) across to last 11{10-9} sts, K 11{10-9}: 87{92-97} sts.

Rows 48-50: Knit across.

Row 51: K5{4-3}, K2 tog, (K5, K2 tog) across to last 10{9-8} sts, K 10{9-8}: 76{80-84} sts.

Rows 52-54: Knit across.

Row 55: K5{4-3}, K2 tog, (K4, K2 tog) across to last 9{8-7} sts, K9{8-7}: 65{68-71} sts.

Row 56: Knit across.

Row 57 (Buttonhole row): K2, YO, K2 tog, knit across.

Rows 58-60: Knit across.

Bind off all sts in knit.

Sew button opposite buttonhole.

Rosy Head Wrap

EASY

Finished Size: 2" wide x 16" long (5 cm x 40.5 cm)

SHOPPING LIST

Yarn (Fine Weight)
- [ ] Peach - 60 yards (55 meters)
- [ ] Brown - 50 yards (45.5 meters)

Knitting Needles
Straight,
- [ ] Size 8 (5 mm)
  or size needed for gauge

Additional Supplies
- [ ] Yarn needle
- [ ] Crochet hook (for fringe ties)

GAUGE INFORMATION
In Garter Stitch (knit every row),
 9 sts and 9 rows = 2" (5 cm)

TECHNIQUES USED
- YO *(Fig. 2, page 29)*
- K2 tog *(Fig. 4, page 29)*
- K3 tog *(Fig. 5, page 29)*

BAND
FIRST END

With Brown and leaving a 6" (15 cm) end, make a slip knot.

Row 1 (Right side)**:** K1.

Row 2: (K, YO, K) **all** in one st: 3 sts.

Row 3: Knit across.

Row 4: K1, (YO, K1) twice: 5 sts.

Row 5: Knit across.

Row 6: K1, YO, K3, YO, K1: 7 sts.

Row 7: Knit across.

Row 8: K1, YO, K5, YO, K1: 9 sts.

Row 9: Knit across.

CENTER SECTION

Knit every row until Band measures approximately 14" (35.5 cm) from cast on edge, ending by working a **wrong** side row.

SECOND END

Row 1: K1, K2 tog, K3, K2 tog, K1: 7 sts.

Row 2: Knit across.

Row 3: K1, (K2 tog, K1) twice: 5 sts.

Row 4: Knit across.

Row 5: K1, K3 tog, K1: 3 sts.

Row 6: Knit across.

Row 7: K3 tog.

Row 8: K1.

Cut yarn leaving a 6" (15 cm) end; draw end through remaining st to secure.

TIES

Cut 12 strands of Brown, each 28" (71 cm) long.

Holding 6 strands together, add fringe as a Tie to cast on stitch of Band *(Figs. 9a & b, page 31)*. Trim ends evenly.

Repeat in bound off stitch with remaining 6 strands.

ROSETTE (Make 3)

With Peach and leaving a long end for sewing, cast on 10 sts.

Row 1 (Right side)**:** Knit across.

Row 2 (Increase row)**:** K1, (YO, K1) across: 19 sts.

Row 3: Knit across.

Rows 4-9: Repeat Rows 2 and 3, 3 times: 145 sts.

Bind off all sts in knit.

Roll cast on edge tightly to form Rosette; thread yarn needle with beginning end and tack base in place. Secure end; do **not** cut yarn. Using photo as a guide for placement and same end, sew each Rosette to Band.

Scoop Neck Top

 EASY

SHOPPING LIST

Yarn (Fine Weight)
[3.5 ounces, 317 yards
(100 grams, 290 meters) per skein]:
☐ {2-2}{3-3-4} skeins

Knitting Needles
Straight,
☐ Size 7 (4.5 mm) **and**
☐ Size 8 (5 mm)
  or sizes needed for gauge

Additional Supplies
☐ Stitch markers
☐ Yarn needle

SIZE INFORMATION

Size: {Small-Medium}
{Large-X Large-2X Large}
Finished Chest Measurement:
{29½-34½}{39½-44½-49½}"/
{75-87.5}{100.5-113-125.5} cm
Length:
{19-20}{21-22-23}"/
{48.5-51}{53.5-56-58.5} cm

Size Note: We have printed the instructions for the sizes in different colors to make it easier for you to find:

• Size Small in Blue
• Size Medium in Pink
• Size Large in Green
• Size X Large in Red
• Size 2X Large in Purple

Instructions in Black apply to all sizes.

GAUGE INFORMATION

With larger size needles,
  in Back pattern,
  15 sts (3 repeats) and
  25 rows = 3¾" (9.5 cm)

TECHNIQUES USED

• M1 *(Figs. 1a & b, page 29)*
• YO *(Fig. 2, page 29)*
• K2 tog *(Fig. 4, page 29)*
• Slip 1 as if to **knit**, K1, PSSO
  (Figs. 6a & b, page 30)

BACK

With smaller size needles,
cast on {61-71}{81-91-101} sts.

Rows 1-6: Knit across.

Change to larger size needles.

Row 7: Knit across.

Row 8 (Right side)**:** K3, K2 tog, (YO, K3, K2 tog) across to last 6 sts, YO, K6.

Row 9: K3, purl across to last 3 sts, K3.

Row 10: K3, YO, slip 1 as if to **knit**, K1, PSSO, ★ K3, YO, slip 1 as if to **knit**, K1, PSSO; repeat from ★ across to last 6 sts, K6.

Row 11: K3, purl across to last 3 sts, K3.

Repeat Rows 8-11 until Back measures approximately {13-13}{14-14½-15}"/{33-33}{35.5-37-38} cm from cast on edge, ending by working Row 11.

Place marker around first and last stitch of last row to mark beginning of Armholes.

Repeat Rows 8-11 until Back measures {18-19}{20-21-22}"/{45.5-48.5}{51-53.5-56} cm from cast on edge, ending by working Row 11.

Change to smaller size needles.

Knit 6 rows.

Bind off all sts in knit.

FRONT

Work same as Back until Front measures approximately {13-13}{14-14½-15}"/{33-33}{35.5-37-38} cm from cast on edge, ending by working Row 11: {61-71}{81-91-101} sts.

Place marker around first and last stitch of last row to mark beginning of armholes.

ARMHOLE & SCOOP NECK SHAPING

Row 1 (Increase row)**:** K3, YO, M1, knit across to last 3 sts, M1, YO, K3: {65-75}{85-95-105} sts.

Rows 2-4: Knit across.

Repeat Rows 1-4 until Front measures {18-19}{20-21-22}"/{45.5-48.5}{51-53.5-56} cm from cast on edge at side edges, ending by working a **wrong** side row.

Change to smaller size needles.

Knit 6 rows.

Bind off all sts in knit.

Sew shoulder seams across bound off edges at each side for {5-5½}{6½-7-8}"/ {12.5-14}{16.5-18-20.5} cm. Weave side seams *(Figs. 8a & b, page 30)*, beginning 3" (7.5 cm) above cast on edge and ending at Armhole markers.

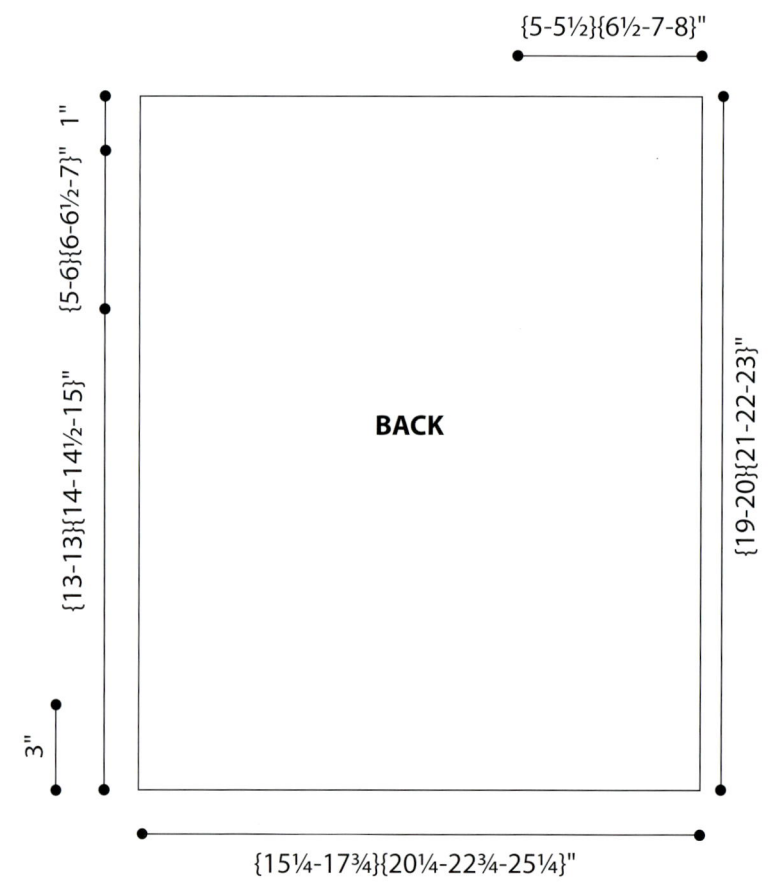

Anchor Pillow

EASY

Finished Size: 13" high x 20½" wide (33 cm x 52 cm)

SHOPPING LIST

Yarn (Medium Weight)

[5 ounces, 256 yards
(141 grams, 234 meters) per skein]:

☐ White - 1 skein
☐ Navy - 1 skein
☐ Red - 1 skein

Knitting Needles

Straight,

☐ Size 10 (6 mm)
   or size needed for gauge

Additional Supplies

☐ Yarn needle
☐ Polyester fiberfill

GAUGE INFORMATION

In Stockinette Stitch
   (knit one row, purl one row),
   12 sts and 16 rows = 4" (10 cm)

FRONT

With White, cast on 60 sts.

Row 1 (Right side)**:** Knit across.

Row 2: Purl across.

Rows 3-50: Repeat Rows 1 and 2, 24 times.

Bind off all sts in knit.

With Navy, using Duplicate Stitch *(Figs. 7a & b, page 30)* and following chart, add design to Front.

KEY

■ - Navy

CHART

BACK

With Navy, cast on 60 sts.

Row 1 (Right side)**:** (K1, P2) across.

Row 2: (K2, P1) across.

Rows 3-50: Repeat Rows 1 and 2, 24 times.

Bind off all sts in pattern.

ASSEMBLY

With **wrong** sides of Front and Back together and matching cast on and bound off edges. Thread yarn needle with two strands of Red. Using photo as a guide for placement, whipstitch edges together inserting needle from **back** to **front** through center of **both** stitches on **both** pieces *(Fig A)*, leaving a 3" (7.5 cm) opening for stuffing, stuff pillow with polyester fiberfill; then whipstitch opening closed.

Fig. A

Striped Tote — EASY

Finished Size: 10" wide x 11" high (25.5 cm x 28 cm)

SHOPPING LIST

Yarn (Medium Weight)
[4 ounces, 203 yards
(113 grams, 186 meters) per skein]:
- ☐ Pink - 2 skeins
- ☐ White - 1 skein
- ☐ Green - 1 skein

Knitting Needles
Straight,
- ☐ Size 10 (6 mm)

  or size needed for gauge

Additional Supplies
- ☐ Yarn needle
- ☐ Bamboo handle with rings - 2

Hold two strands of yarn together throughout. To work with two strands of White **or** Green, hold strands from the center and the outside of the skein.

GAUGE INFORMATION
In Stockinette Stitch
(knit one row, purl one row),
12 sts and 16 rows = 4" (10 cm)

PANEL (Make 2)
With Pink and beginning at top edge, cast on 32 sts.

Rows 1 and 2: (K2, P2) across.

Rows 3 and 4: (P2, K2) across.

Rows 5 and 6: (K2, P2) across.

Row 7 (Right side)**:** Purl across.

Rows 8 and 9: Knit across.

Row 10: Purl across; cut Pink.

Row 11: With White, knit across.

Row 12: Purl across.

Cut White.

Rows 13 and 14: With Green, repeat Rows 11 and 12.

Cut Green.

Rows 15 and 16: With Pink, repeat Rows 11 and 12.

Cut Pink.

Rows 17 and 18: Repeat Rows 11 and 12.

Cut White.

Rows 19 and 20: With Green, repeat Rows 11 and 12.

Cut Green.

With Pink and beginning with a **knit** row, work in Stotckinette Stitch until piece measures approximately 11" (28 cm) from cast on edge, ending by working a **purl** row.

Bind off all sts in knit.

With **wrong** sides together and matching stripes, weave side seams and bottom edge with one strand of Pink *(Figs. 8a, c & d, pages 30 & 31)*.

With Pink, sew handles to **wrong** side of Row 1.

Long Vest — EASY

Finished Size: 40½" width x 34" length (103 cm x 86.5 cm)

SHOPPING LIST

Yarn (Medium Weight)
[3.5 ounces, 186 yards
(100 grams, 170 meters) per skein]:
☐ 4 skeins

Knitting Needles
Straight,
☐ Size 11 (8 mm)
or size needed for gauge

GAUGE INFORMATION

In pattern,
  8 sts (2 repeats) = 3¼" (8.25 cm);
  13 rows = 3½" (9 cm)

TECHNIQUES USED

- YO *(Fig. 2, page 29)*
- Adding new sts *(Figs. 3a & b, page 29)*
- K2 tog *(Fig. 4, page 29)*

Each row is worked across the length of the Body.

BODY

Cast on 84 sts.

Row 1: (K1, P1) across.

Row 2: (P1, K1) across.

Rows 3 and 4: Repeat Rows 1 and 2.

Row 5: (K1, P1) 3 times, (YO, K2 tog) across to last 6 sts, (K1, P1) 3 times.

Row 6: (P1, K1) 3 times, purl across to last 5 sts, K1, (P1, K1) twice.

Row 7: (K1, P1) 3 times, knit across to last 5 sts, P1, (K1, P1) twice.

Row 8: (P1, K1) 3 times, purl across to last 5 sts, K1, (P1, K1) twice.

Row 9: (K1, P1) 3 times, (K2, YO, K2 tog) across to last 6 sts, (K1, P1) 3 times.

Rows 10-12: Repeat Rows 6-8.

Row 13: (K1, P1) 3 times, YO, K2 tog, (K2, YO, K2 tog) across to last 8 sts, K3, P1, (K1, P1) twice.

Rows 14-46: Repeat Rows 6-13, 4 times; then repeat Row 6 once **more**.

Row 47: (K1, P1) 3 times, K 12, bind off next 24 sts (**armhole begun**), knit across to last 5 sts, P1, (K1, P1) twice: 60 sts.

Row 48: (P1, K1) 3 times, P 36, **turn**; add on 24 sts (**armhole finished**), **turn**; P 13, K1, (P1, K1) twice: 84 sts.

Row 49: (K1, P1) 3 times, (K2, YO, K2 tog) 3 times, K 24, (K2, YO, K2 tog) across to last 6 sts, (K1, P1) 3 times.

Rows 50-53: Repeat Rows 10-13.

Rows 54-102: Repeat Rows 6-9, 12 times; then repeat Row 6 once **more**.

Rows 103-105: Repeat Rows 47-49.

Rows 106-146: Repeat Rows 6-13, 5 times; then repeat Row 6 once **more**.

Row 147: (K1, P1) 3 times, (YO, K2 tog) across to last 6 sts, (K1, P1) 3 times.

Row 148: (P1, K1) across.

Row 149: (K1, P1) across.

Rows 150 and 151: Repeat Rows 148 and 149.

Bind off all sts in pattern.

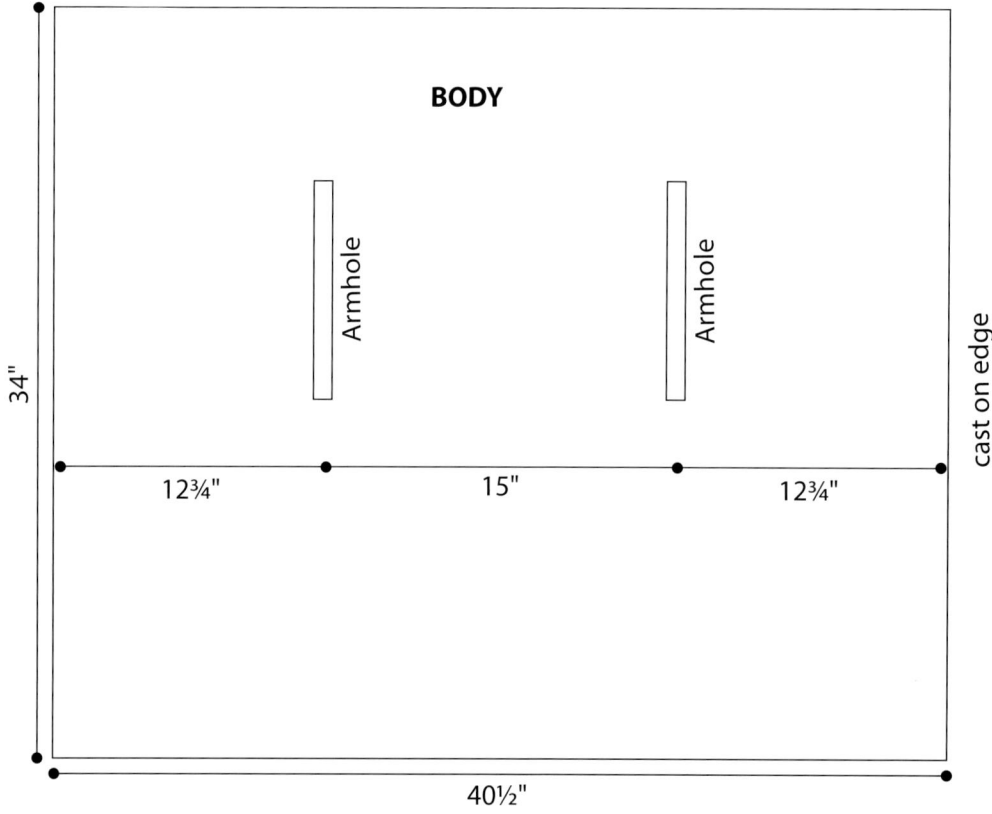

Surfside Tunic

 EASY

SHOPPING LIST

Yarn (Light Weight)
[3.5 ounces, 230 yards
(100 grams, 210 meters) per hank]:
☐ 3{4-4} hanks

Knitting Needles
Straight,
☐ Size 10 (6 mm)
 or size needed for gauge

Additional Supplies
☐ Yarn needle

SIZE INFORMATION

Size: Small {Medium-Large}
Panel Width:
24½{27¼-30}"/62{69-76} cm
Length:
23½{23½-26}"/59.5{59.5-66} cm

Size Note: We have printed the instructions for the sizes in different colors to make it easier for you to find:

• Size Small in Blue
• Size Medium in Pink
• Size Large in Green

Instructions in Black apply to all sizes.

GAUGE INFORMATION

In pattern,
   11 sts = 4" (10 cm);
   Rows 1-11 = 3" (7.5 cm)

TECHNIQUES USED

- YO twice *(Fig. B, page 2)*

Each row is worked across the length of the Panel.

PANEL (Make 2)

Cast on 65{65-71} sts.

Row 1 (Right side)**:** Knit across.

Rows 2 and 3: K3, purl across to last 3 sts, K3.

Row 4: Knit across.

Row 5: K3, YO twice as you knit next 59{59-65} sts, K3: 124{124-136} sts.

To elongate stitches, purl only the first YO of each stitch, dropping the remaining YO from the left needle. Tug gently on the piece to even the elongated stitches.

Row 6: K3, elongating each st purl across to last 3 sts, K3: 65{65-71} sts.

Row 7: Knit across.

Row 8: K3, purl across to last 3 sts, K3.

Rows 9 and 10: Knit across.

Rows 11 and 12: K3, purl across to last 3 sts, K3.

Row 13: Knit across.

Row 14: K3, purl across to last 3 sts, K3.

Row 15: K3, YO twice as you knit next 59{59-65} sts, K3: 124{124-136} sts.

Row 16: K3, elongating each st purl across to last 3 sts, K3: 65{65-71} sts.

Rows 17 thru 86{96-106}: Repeat Rows 7-16, 7{8-9} times.

Next Row: K3, purl across to last 3 sts, K3.

Next 2 Rows: Knit across.

Last Row: K3, purl across to last 3 sts, K3.

Bind off all sts in knit.

ASSEMBLY

With **right** sides of Panels facing and cast on and bound off edges together.

Weave shoulder seams *(Figs. 8a & b, page 30)*, leaving a 12{15-17}"/30.5{38-43} cm neck opening.

Weave side seams, beginning 9" (23 cm) down from shoulder seam and ending 7" (18 cm) above bottom edge *(Figs. 8c & d, page 31)*.

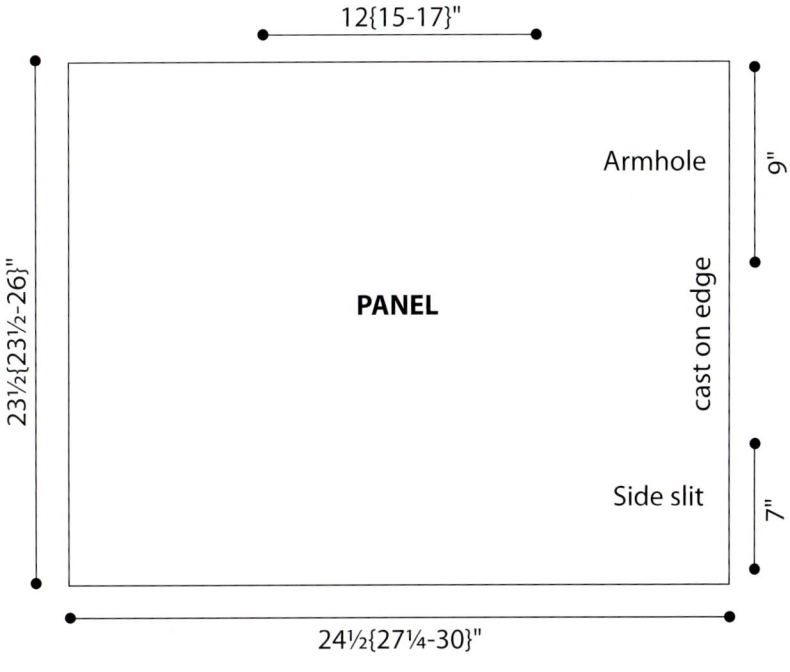

Fringed Hip Wrap ▪▪▫▫ EASY

SHOPPING LIST

Yarn (Fine Weight) 🧶2
[2.29 ounces, 185 yards
(65 grams, 169 meters) per skein]:
☐ 3{3-4} skeins

Knitting Needles
Straight,
☐ Size 8 (5 mm)
  or size needed for gauge

Additional Supplies
☐ Crochet hook (for fringe)

SIZE INFORMATION
Size: Small {Medium-Large}
Finished Waist Measurement:
28{31½-35}"/71{80-89} cm
Length: 14" (35.5 cm)

Size Note: We have printed the instructions for the sizes in different colors to make it easier for you to find:

• Size Small in Blue
• Size Medium in Pink
• Size Large in Green

Instructions in Black apply to all sizes.

GAUGE INFORMATION

In pattern,
   11 sts (one repeat) = 3¾" (9.5 cm);
   18 rows = 4" (10 cm)

TECHNIQUES USED

- YO *(Fig. 2, page 29)*
- K2 tog *(Fig. 4, page 29)*
- Slip 1 as if to **knit**, K1, PSSO
  (Figs. 6a & b, page 30)

Each row is worked across the width of the Body.

BODY

Cast on 41 sts.

Rows 1-5: Knit across.

Row 6 AND ALL EVEN-NUMBERED ROWS: K3, purl across to last 3, K3.

Row 7 (Right side): ★ K9, YO, slip 1 as if to **knit**, K1, PSSO; repeat from ★ 2 times **more**, K8.

Row 9: K7, K2 tog, YO, K1, YO, slip 1 as if to **knit**, K1, PSSO, ★ K6, K2 tog, YO, K1, YO, slip 1 as if to **knit**, K1, PSSO; repeat from ★ once **more**, K7.

Row 11: K6, K2 tog, YO, K3, YO, slip 1 as if to **knit**, K1, PSSO, ★ K4, K2 tog, YO, K3, YO, slip 1 as if to **knit**, K1, PSSO; repeat from ★ once **more**, K6.

Row 13: K5, K2 tog, YO, K5, YO, slip 1 as if to **knit**, K1, PSSO, ★ K2, K2 tog, YO, K5, YO, slip 1 as if to **knit**, K1, PSSO; repeat from ★ once **more**, K5.

Rows 15 thru 126{142-158}: Repeat Rows 7-14, 14{16-18} times.

Last 5 rows: Knit across.

Bind off all sts in knit.

FRINGE

Holding 2 strands of yarn together, each 18" (45.5 cm) long, add fringe evenly spaced across one long edge of Wrap (bottom edge) *(Figs. 9a & b, page 31)*. Trim ends evenly.

TIES

Cut 18 strands of yarn, each 40" (101.5 cm) long.

Holding 3 strands together, add fringe in first 3 cast on sts at top edge.

Using the 3 groups of fringe, braid strands until Tie measures approximately 11" (28 cm); then overhand knot strands together. Trim ends evenly.

Repeat on last 3 bound off sts at top edge.

General Instructions

ABBREVIATIONS

cm	centimeters
K	knit
M1	make one
mm	millimeters
P	purl
PSSO	pass slipped stitch over
st(s)	stitch(es)
tog	together
YO	yarn over

KNIT TERMINOLOGY	
UNITED STATES	INTERNATIONAL
gauge =	tension
bind off =	cast off
yarn over (YO) =	yarn forward (yfwd) **or** yarn around needle (yrn)

SYMBOLS & TERMS

★ — work instructions following ★ as many **more** times as indicated in addition to the first time.

( ) or [ ] — work enclosed instructions **as many** times as specified by the number immediately following **or** work all enclosed instructions in the stitch indicated **or** contains explanatory remarks.

colon (:) — the number(s) given after a colon at the end of a row denote(s) the number of stitches you should have on that row.

GAUGE

Exact gauge is **essential** for proper size. Before beginning your project, make a sample swatch with the yarn and needle specified. After completing the swatch, measure it, counting your stitches and rows carefully. If your swatch is larger or smaller than specified, **make another, changing needle size to get the correct gauge**. Keep trying until you find the size needles that will give you the specified gauge.

Yarn Weight Symbol & Names	LACE 0	SUPER FINE 1	FINE 2	LIGHT 3	MEDIUM 4	BULKY 5	SUPER BULKY 6	JUMBO 7
Type of Yarns in Category	Fingering, size 10 crochet thread	Sock, Fingering, Baby	Sport, Baby	DK, Light Worsted	Worsted, Afghan, Aran	Chunky, Craft, Rug	Super Bulky, Roving	Jumbo, Roving
Knit Gauge Ranges in Stockinette St to 4" (10 cm)	33-40 sts**	27-32 sts	23-26 sts	21-24 sts	16-20 sts	12-15 sts	7-11 sts	6 sts and fewer
Advised Needle Size Range	000 to 1	1 to 3	3 to 5	5 to 7	7 to 9	9 to 11	11 to 17	17 and larger

* GUIDELINES ONLY: The chart above reflects the most commonly used gauges and needle sizes for specific yarn categories.

** Lace weight yarns are usually knitted on larger needles to create lacy openwork patterns. Accordingly, a gauge range is difficult to determine. Always follow the gauge stated in your pattern.

■□□□ BEGINNER	Projects for first-time knitters using basic knit and purl stitches. Minimal shaping.
■■□□ EASY	Projects using basic stitches, repetitive stitch patterns, simple color changes, and simple shaping and finishing.
■■■□ INTERMEDIATE	Projects with a variety of stitches, such as basic cables and lace, simple intarsia, double-pointed needles and knitting in the round needle techniques, mid-level shaping and finishing.
■■■■ EXPERIENCED	Projects using advanced techniques and stitches, such as short rows, fair isle, more intricate intarsia, cables, lace patterns, and numerous color changes.

INCREASES
MAKE ONE (abbreviated M1)
Insert the **left** needle under the horizontal strand between the stitches from the **front** *(Fig. 1a)*. Then knit into the **back** of the strand *(Fig. 1b)*.

Fig. 1a

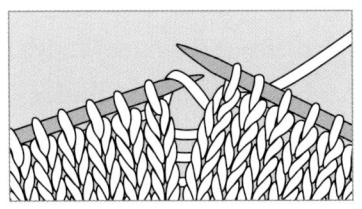

Fig. 1b

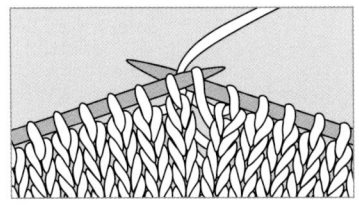

YARN OVER *(abbreviated YO)*
Bring the yarn forward **between** the needles, then back **over** the top of the right hand needle, so that it is now in position to knit the next stitch *(Fig. 2)*.

Fig. 2

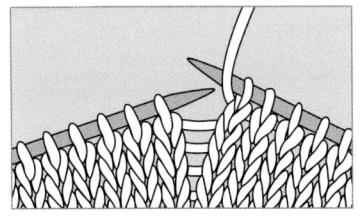

ADDING NEW STITCHES
Insert the right needle into stitch on left needle as if to **knit**, yarn over and pull loop through *(Fig. 3a)*, insert the left needle into the loop just worked from **front** to **back** and slip the loop onto the left needle *(Fig. 3b)*. Repeat for required number of stitches.

Fig. 3a

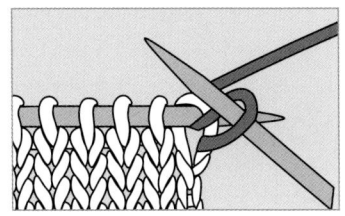

Fig. 3b

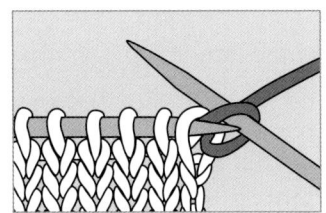

DECREASES
KNIT 2 TOGETHER
(abbreviated K2 tog)
Insert the right needle into the **front** of the first two stitches on the left needle as if to **knit** *(Fig. 4)*, then **knit** them together as if they were one stitch.

Fig. 4

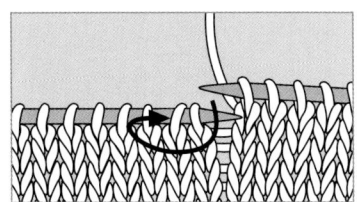

KNIT 3 TOGETHER
(abbreviated K3 tog)
Insert the right needle into the **front** of the first three stitches on the left needle as if to **knit** *(Fig. 5)*, then **knit** them together as if they were one stitch.

Fig. 5

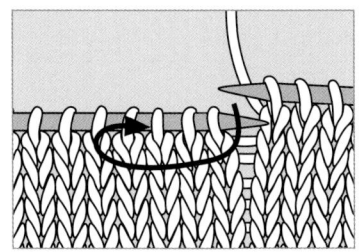

KNITTING NEEDLES		
UNITED STATES	ENGLISH U.K.	METRIC (mm)
0	13	2
1	12	2.25
2	11	2.75
3	10	3.25
4	9	3.5
5	8	3.75
6	7	4
7	6	4.5
8	5	5
9	4	5.5
10	3	6
10½	2	6.5
11	1	8
13	00	9
15	000	10
17	---	12.75
19	---	15
35	---	19
50	---	25

SLIP 1, KNIT 1, PASS SLIPPED STITCH OVER

(abbreviated slip 1, K1, PSSO)

Slip one stitch as if to **knit** *(Fig. 6a)*. Knit the next stitch. With the left needle, bring the slipped stitch over the knit stitch *(Fig. 6b)* and off the needle.

Fig. 6a **Fig. 6b**

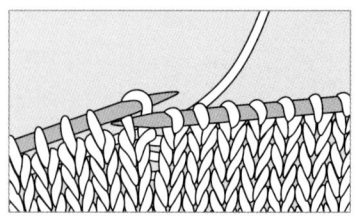
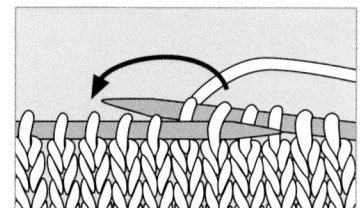

DUPLICATE STITCH

Duplicate Stitch is worked on Stockinette Stitch. Each knit stitch forms a V and you want to completely cover that V so that the design appears to have been knit into the piece. Each square on a chart represents one knit stitch that is to be covered by Duplicate Stitch.

Thread a yarn needle with an 18" (45.5 cm) length of yarn. Beginning at lower right of the design and with **right** side facing, bring the needle up from the **wrong** side at the base of the V leaving an end to be woven in later (never tie knots). The needle should always go **between** the strands of yarn. Follow the **right** side of the V up and insert the needle from **right** to **left** under the legs of the V immediately above it, keeping the yarn on top of the stitch *(Fig. 7a)*, and draw through. Follow the left side of the V back down to the base and insert the needle back through the bottom of the same stitch where the first stitch began *(Fig. 7b, Duplicate Stitch completed)*.

Continuing to follow chart, bring needle up through the next stitch. Repeat for each stitch, keeping even tension of knit fabric to avoid puckering. When a length of yarn is finished, run it under several stitches on back of work to secure.

Fig. 7a **Fig. 7b**

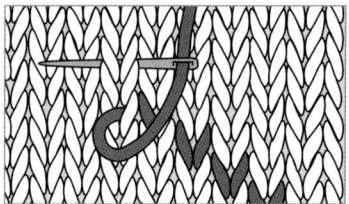

WEAVING SEAMS

Weaving can be used to join the ends of rows or the cast on/bound off edges of two pieces in a manner that appears to be seamless.

ENDS OF ROWS

With the **right** side of both pieces facing you and edges even, sew through both sides once to secure the seam. Insert the needle under the bar **between** the first and second stitches on the row and pull the yarn through *(Fig. 8a)* **or** through one strand on each piece *(Fig. 8b)*. Insert the needle under the next bar **or** strand on the second side. Repeat from side to side, being careful to match rows. If the edges are different lengths, it may be necessary to insert the needle under two bars at one edge.

Fig. 8a

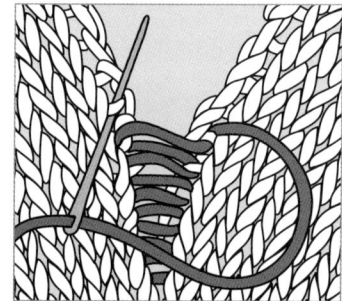

Fig. 8b

CAST ON/BOUND OFF EDGES

With the **right** side of both pieces facing you and matching the cast on/bound off edges, bring the yarn needle from behind the work and through the center of the first stitch. ★ Bring the yarn needle over the top of the stitches and insert it under both loops on the second side *(Fig. 8c)*. Bring the yarn needle back over the cast on stitches and insert it under the inverted V of the next stitch *(Fig. 8d)*. Repeat from ★ across. Pull the yarn gently every 2 or 3 stitches, being careful to maintain even tension.

Fig. 8c

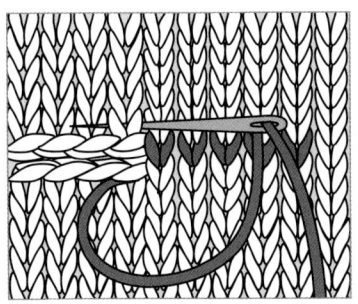

Fig. 8d

FRINGE

Cut a piece of cardboard 8" (20.5 cm) wide and half as long as specified in individual instructions for strands. Wind the yarn **loosely** and **evenly** around the cardboard lengthwise until the card is filled, then cut across one end; repeat as needed.

Hold together as many strands as specified in individual instructions; fold in half.

With **wrong** side facing and using a crochet hook, draw the folded end up around a stitch **or** through a stitch and pull the loose ends through the folded end *(Fig. 9a)*; draw the knot up **tightly** *(Fig. 9b)*. Repeat, spacing as specified in individual instructions.

Lay flat on a hard surface and trim the ends.

Fig. 9a   **Fig. 9b**

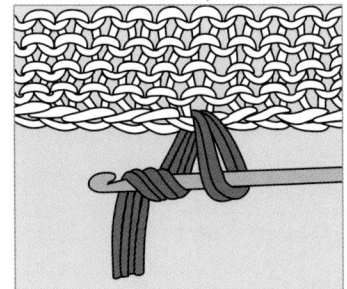 

Meet Kristi Simpson

Inspired by her love of yarn, Kristi Simpson creates crochet and knit patterns with a fresh and modern touch. The mother of five became hooked on crochet after teaching herself so she could help her daughter make a scarf from a "learn to crochet" kit that was a gift.

"I was amazed that I could take a string of yarn and create something so useful and pretty," she says. "Needless to say, I never stopped!"

For more about Kristi's widely published designs, visit kristisimpson.net or find her on Ravelry, Facebook, and Pinterest.

Yarn Information

The items in this book were made using a variety of yarns. Any brand of the specific weight of yarn may be used. It is best to refer to the yardage/meters when determining how many balls or skeins to purchase. Remember, to achieve the finished size, it is the GAUGE/TENSION that is important, not the brand of yarn.

For your convenience, listed below are the specific yarns used to create our photography models. Because yarn manufacturers make frequent changes to their product lines, you may sometimes find it necessary to use a substitute yarn or to search for the discontinued product at alternate suppliers (locally or online).

BAREFOOT SANDALS
Lion Brand® 24/7 Cotton®
#178 Jade

SEASIDE COASTERS
Lion Brand® 24/7 Cotton®
Red - #113 Red
Navy - #110 Navy
White - #100 White
Yellow - #157 Lemon

LACY CAPE
Lion Brand® 24/7 Cotton®
#156 Mint

ROSY HEAD WRAP
Premier Yarns® Cotton Fair®
Peach - #27-07 Bright Peach
Brown - #27-16 Cocoa

SCOOP NECK TOP
Premier Yarns® Cotton Fair®
#27-04 Turquoise

ANCHOR PILLOW
Red Heart® Soft®
White - #4600 White
Navy - #4604 Navy
Red - #5142 Cherry Red

STRIPED TOTE
Premier® Yarns Deborah Norville™ Collection Everyday® Soft Worsted
Pink - #100-26 Grenadine
White - #100-01 Snow White
Green - #100-16 Kiwi

LONG VEST
Lion Brand® 24/7 Cotton®
#098 Ecru

SURFSIDE TUNIC
Universal Yarns® Cotton Supreme DK Seaspray
#303 Bright Honeydew

FRINGED HIP WRAP
Premier® Yarns Deborah Norville Collection™ Serenity® Garden™
#800-23 Bouquet

We have made every effort to ensure that these instructions are accurate and complete. We cannot, however, be responsible for human error, typographical mistakes, or variations in individual work.

Production Team: Instructional/ Technical Editor - Lois J. Long; Editorial Writer - Susan Frantz Wlles; Senior Graphic Artist - Lora Puls; Graphic Artist - Lora Puls; Photo Stylist - Lori Wenger; and Photographer - Jason Masters.

Copyright © 2017 by Leisure Arts, Inc., 104 Champs Blvd., STE 100, Maumelle, AR 72113-6738. All rights reserved. This publication is protected under federal copyright laws. Reproduction or distribution of this publication or any other Leisure Arts publication, including publications which are out of print, is prohibited unless specifically authorized. This includes, but is not limited to, any form of reproduction or distribution on or through the Internet, including posting, scanning, or e-mail transmission.